Sing Pop
A Cappella

Book Two

T0084526

CD Tracklisting

1-5   **All I Have To Do Is Dream**
(Bryant)
Sony/ATV Music Publishing (UK) Limited

6-10   **Happy Together**
(Gordon/Bonner)
Windswept Trio Music Company Limited/Robbins Music Corporation Limited

11-15   **House Of The Rising Sun**
(Traditional/Partington)
Novello & Company Limited

16-20   **Lovely Day**
(Withers/Scarborough)
Warner/Chappell Music Limited/Chelsea Music Publishing Company Limited

21-25   **Man In The Mirror**
(Ballard/Garrett)
Universal/MCA Music Limited/Cherry Lane Music Limited

Published by
Novello Publishing Limited
14-15 Berners Street,
London W1T 3LJ, UK.

Exclusive Distributors:
Music Sales Limited
Distribution Centre, Newmarket Road,
Bury St Edmunds, Suffolk IP33 3YB, UK.
Music Sales Pty Limited
20 Resolution Drive, Caringbah,
NSW 2229, Australia.

Order No. NOV161568
ISBN 978-1-84938-621-0

This book © 2010 Novello & Company Limited.

Unauthorised reproduction of any part of this
publication by any means including photocopying is an
infringement of copyright.

Cover Design by Ruth Keating.

Printed in the EU.

Your Guarantee of Quality
As publishers, we strive to produce every book to the
highest commercial standards.
This book has been carefully designed to minimise awkward
page turns and to make playing from it a real pleasure.
Particular care has been given to specifying acid-free, neutral-sized paper
made from pulps which have not been elemental chlorine bleached.
This pulp is from farmed sustainable forests and was
produced with special regard for the environment.
Throughout, the printing and binding have been planned to
ensure a sturdy, attractive publication which should give years of enjoyment.
If your copy fails to meet our high standards,
please inform us and we will gladly replace it.

www.chesternovello.com

Sing Pop
A Cappella

Book Two

Introduction

Some people find it hard to understand how anyone can be a musician without being able to sight-read music. Even so, I know many gifted and talented musicians who cannot read a note. There is no reason for anyone to feel insecure because they cannot read music; sight-reading is undoubtedly a skill useful at all levels of music-making, but not possessing that skill should never exclude anyone from the music-making experience. In an age when digital recorders are often available on phones, PDAs and iPods, there are always other ways of setting down music. Some people even devise their own notation system.

When it comes to transmitting music to other people who may not sight-read well or at all, the traditional practice of 'note bashing' on a piano is something with which many will be familiar. It does the job but arguably it emphasises the 'note value' of the music at the expense of conveying any feeling for, or understanding of the piece; usually these issues are intended to be addressed later.

Personally I found it a revelation when people began to teach me songs not by bashing piano notes, but by singing a line to me and getting me to sing it back several times: no notation but lots of repetition. This method makes teaching songs an option for anyone who can sing and communicate well. That in turn means many singers who do not possess the traditional qualifications of accompaniment and sight-reading skills can still take on the role of choral director. They do not even need a great voice, just an ability to sing in tune and convey the feel of the music.

As I am teaching a song, I indicate the pitch and rhythm with gestures, so adding visual information to the sound. This approach lends itself particularly well to the kinaesthetic learner who usually responds positively to being involved in some form of physical activity and is happy to join in all aspects of this 'call-and-response' process. By contrast those who struggle most with learning songs by ear are those who have been exposed to sight-reading much too early and have consequently almost lost their auditory skills. Fortunately they too can re-learn and in my experience they often discover that it is very satisfying to be reconnected with learning by ear.

One consequence of the growth of teaching/learning by ear has been a rise in popularity of the youth choir and a cappella communities. With many singers feeling more confident about attempting to teach and lead others, the only caveat is that they must be prepared to learn all of the parts of each song themselves before attempting to teach them. One compromise is to appoint a leader per part, which can lighten the load for less experienced leaders.

Almost all my groups work on the 'Comprehensive School' ideal that by mixing very experienced singers with beginners, everyone benefits and we create a true community of singers. There is no audition policy and no requirement to be able to read music. People who have not sung for decades are sandwiched between self-assured and practised singers, and within a matter of weeks their singing and confidence improves beyond measure.

Organising singing sessions requires little in the way of premises and equipment. I like to have enough chairs for the entire group and a wall where I can Blu-Tack sheets of paper or project images from my laptop so everyone can see the words without clutching sheets. The first time I teach an arrangement, I have some form of notation with me, but in general I prefer to memorise it and teach without it as I tend to use my arms and whole body to indicate pitch rhythm and intonation.

Novello Publishing Limited
part of The Music Sales Group
London / New York / Paris / Sydney / Copenhagen / Berlin / Madrid / Hong Kong / Tokyo

A Little Bit on Voice Care

This is not a voice care book, however teaching a cappella can be much harder on the voice. If you are teaching alone you will be using a large range. Remember, you do not always have to sing loud since even in a big space people tend to listen carefully to quiet singing. This means you can use different qualities in your voice as you alternate between loud and soft singing.

Both male and female teachers will face some difficulties singing parts out of their natural range. I will sing bass an octave higher which to me feels as if I am singing in the same place as a bass. For a man teaching all sections of a choir I would suggest that when singing soprano and alto he sings an octave lower if it feels comfortable to do so – falsetto can be hard on the voice if you are singing for any length of time.

The Songs

This book covers some of my popular a cappella arrangements. They have all been tried and tested by singing groups of various ages and numbers. I believe that anyone who is confident that they can sing in time and in tune – and feels enthusiastic about teaching a group – should go for it. The songs range from simple to fairly challenging and I have included notes on experiences I have had when teaching them in the hope that these might prove useful to others.

I certainly don't want to discourage more traditional choirs from dipping into this book. Many of these songs and arrangements can offer a lovely contrast within a programme of classical/traditional pieces. I also believe it is desirable for a choir that spends a lot of time learning from notation to take a break and learn something by ear.

Each song in the book is covered by five tracks on the CD. The first is a full performance; and the remaining four tracks each focus on one of the vocal parts (soprano, alto, tenor, bass). In these performances, the relevant part will feature more prominently, allowing the singer to learn their part more effectively. Experience shows that the practice CDs are very popular. Many choir members like to play them in the car or on iPods when commuting. They enjoy learning their parts by being immersed in the music.

All I Have To Do Is Dream
Felice and Boudleaux Bryant

We all love to sing songs that we have been hearing all our lives and believe we already know. In practice the melody will usually need to be re-learned so that everyone is singing it the same. *All I Have To Do Is Dream* is such a song. The tenor part is a new melody, which just lifts the whole arrangement, so it sounds a bit fresh, and gives the tenors a chance to sparkle. My choirs have women and men singing tenor and so usually I tend to keep the tenor parts just a little higher so they can be comfortably sung by both. The altos are delighted that they get to sing the tune! With a really well-known song I find it is a good idea not to start with the familiar tune: if your singers are not experienced they can get distracted by a well-known melody. I might try teaching bass, alto and then soprano followed by the other tune the tenors sing, which weaves in between the old melody. I might teach the tenor part first as it is a new tune altogether.

Happy Together
The Turtles

The lovely thing about this arrangement is you can be singing it in three parts in a matter of minutes. In the verse the bass is four notes moving down in steps: D, C, B♭, A. We sing each note eight times, all on the beat to form the bass line. The places where the little riff (first sung by the tenors) goes up and down can be indicated with hand gestures... but you do need to know it before you teach it! The tune goes on top. When teaching the gaps in tunes (in this case 'Imagine you and me-gap-I do-gap-I think about you day and night-gap-it's only right-gap') I might get people to put in a grunt, a clap, a stamp or a gesture to remind them of the spaces (these are to be taken out later). Everyone gets a turn singing the tune, the bass, and the riff. The solo section is almost the same notes as the chorus – usually the first note of each bar extended. If you wish you can simplify the whole thing by just keeping each part doing the same thing all the way through.

House Of The Rising Sun
Traditional

I usually teach all the parts of the intro first and 'walk it round the room'. The rest of the song's character and feel is then clear. The tune stays in the soprano throughout and the backings share the same rhythm. It can help to have the sopranos sing their part quietly as each of the other parts learns its own section, so everybody can feel how the parts fit together. There are some nice 'clashy' bits where two parts sing notes that are very close together. It is worth isolating these sections (for example bar 71, 1'40" audio) where the sopranos sing an E, and the alto a D. Singling them out makes it clear to the singers that it's dissonant but not wrong!

Lovely Day
Bill Withers

Verse 1 is sung by soprano and alto, verse 2 by tenor and bass. This can stay the same all the way through if you find it easier. If the tenors and basses sing verse 2 then the return to the line 'then I look at you' will need focussing on. Also in the intro the soprano, alto and tenor riffs can be left out and everyone can just learn the bass. The links are the places to focus on, especially when the basses and tenors move from the verse riff to the middle riff.

Man In The Mirror
Glen Ballard and Siedah Garrett

Learning this song is not for the faint-hearted, but it's well worth it – a glorious sing! *Man In The Mirror* is best taught in chunks over several sessions. Strong tenors (or even a mic'd up soloist) are needed for the verses. Once again the backings should be taught first. This is a song where the practice CD really does come into its own and singers should be encouraged to listen to it as often as possible prior to a learning session.

All I Have To Do Is Dream

Words & Music by Boudleaux Bryant
Arranged by Gitika Partington

© Copyright 1958 Sony/ATV Music Publishing (UK) Limited.
All Rights Reserved. International Copyright Secured.

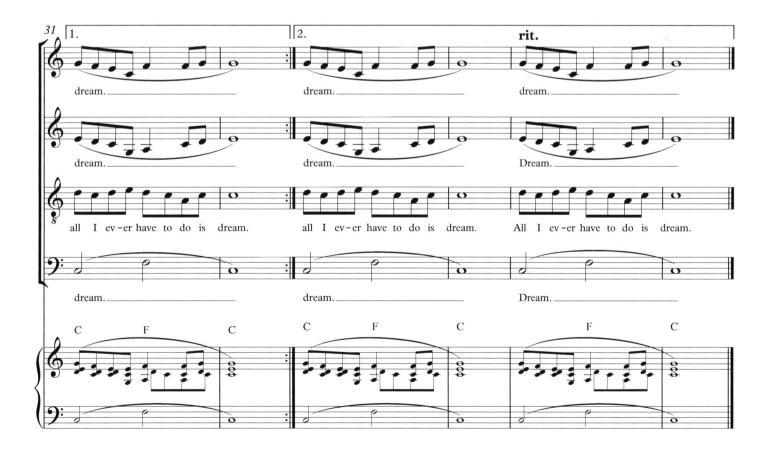

Happy Together

Words & Music by Alan Gordon & Garry Bonner
Arranged by Gitika Partington

© Copyright 1967 Trio Music Company Incorporated/Alley Music Corporation, USA.
Windswept Trio Music Company Limited (50%)/Robbins Music Corporation Limited (50%).
All Rights Reserved. International Copyright Secured.

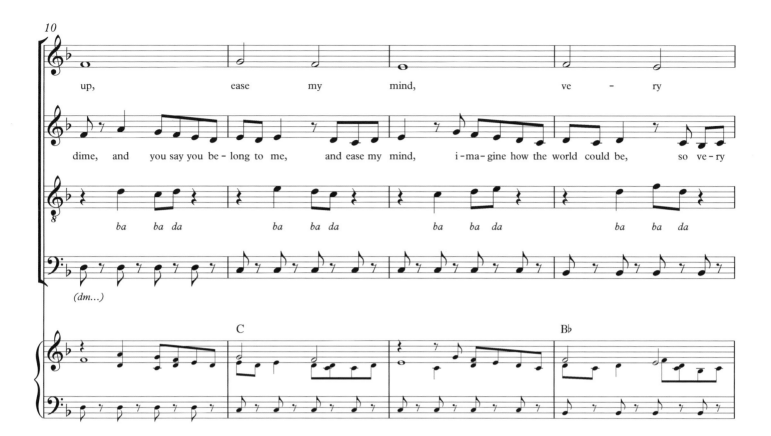

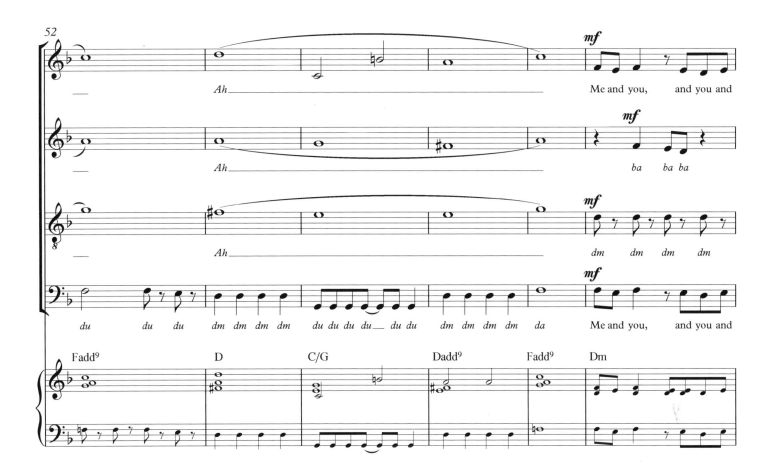

House Of The Rising Sun

Traditional
Arranged by Gitika Partington

© Copyright 2010 Novello & Company Limited.
All Rights Reserved. International Copyright Secured.

Lovely Day

Words & Music by Bill Withers & Skip Scarborough
Arranged by Gitika Partington

© Copyright 1977, 1978 Unichappell Music Incorporated/Golden Withers Music, USA.
Warner/Chappell Music Limited/Chelsea Music Publishing Company Limited.
All Rights Reserved. International Copyright Secured.

VERSE 1

And some-thing with-out warn - ing, love,_ bears hea-vy on my mind.

And some-thing with-out warn - ing, love,_ bears hea-vy on my mind.

ba ba ba ba da ba da da ba ba ba ba da ba da da ba ba ba da ba ba ba ba ba ba ba

ba ba ba ba da ba da da ba ba ba ba da ba da da ba ba ba da ba ba ba ba ba ba ba

E   C#m⁷   Amaj⁷   C D/B

MIDDLE

Then I look at you and the world's al - right with me.____ Oh,

Then I look at you and the world's al - right with me.____ Oh,

Then I look at you and the world's al - right with me. Oh,

ba ba ba ba__ ba ba ba ba ba ba ba__ ba ba ba ba ba ba ba__ ba ba ba ba ba ba ba__

C/D   D/E   Am⁷   Bm⁷

just one look at you __ and I know it's gon-na be __ a love-ly

just one look at you __ and I know it's gon-na be, __

just one look at you __ and I know it's gon-na be __ a love-ly

ba ba ba ba ba ba ba ba ba ba and I know it's gon-na be, __

C/D   D/E   Am⁷   B⁷

CHORUS 1

day, __ a love-ly

love-ly day, love-ly day, love-ly day, love-ly day, love-ly day, love-ly day, love-ly day, love-ly day, a love-ly

day, __ a love-ly

ba ba ba ba da ba da da ba ba ba ba da ba da da ba ba ba da ba ba ba da ba da ba

E   C#m⁷   Amaj⁷   C   D/B

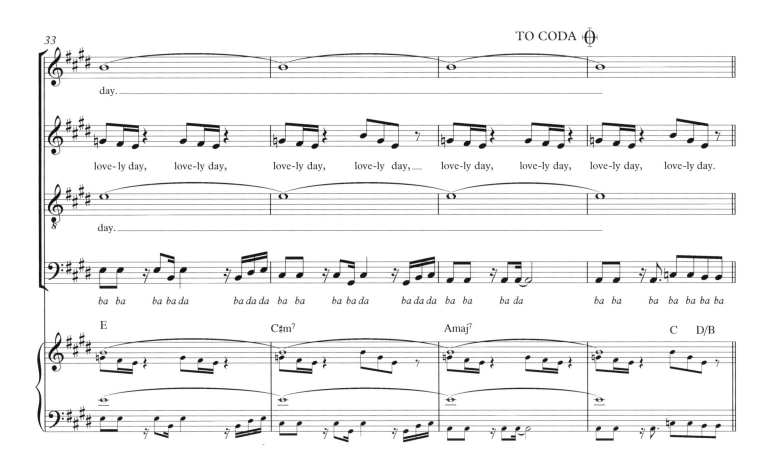

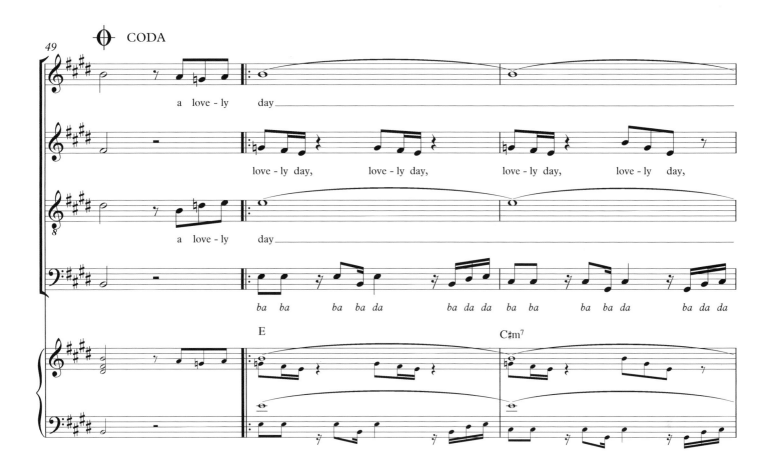

Man In The Mirror

Words & Music by Glen Ballard & Siedah Garrett
Arranged by Gitika Partington

© Copyright 1987 Aerostation Corporation, USA/Yellow Brick Road Music, USA.
Universal/MCA Music Limited (50%) (administered in Germany by Universal/MCA Music Publ. GmbH.)/Cherry Lane Music Limited (50%).
All Rights Reserved. International Copyright Secured.

I'm ask-ing him to change his ways_ and no_ mes-sage could have been a - ny clear-er, if you

I'm ask-ing him to change his ways_ and no mes-sage could have been a - ny clear-er, if you

ask - ing_ him to change his ways_ and no_ mes-sage could have been a - ny clear-er, if you

ask - ing_ him to change his ways, no mes - sage could be a - ny clear-er, if you

wan-na make the world a bet-ter place take a look at your-self and then make a change. na na na na na na_ na na

wan-na make the world a bet-ter place take a look at your-self and then make a change._ na na na na na na_ na na

wan-na make the world a bet-ter place take a look at your-self and then make a change._ na na na na na na_ na na

wan-na make the world a bet-ter place take a look at your-self and then make a change._____ na na_ na_

na na na na___ na na na Vic - tim, vic - tim___ of sel - - - fish

na na na na___ na na na Vic - tim, vic - tim___ of sel - - - fish

na na na na___ na na na I've been a vic-tim of___ a sel-fish kind of love, it's time that I re-a - lise___

___ na na na Vic - tim, vic - tim___ of sel - fish___ love,

love, no home, nick - el to loan, could it be rea-lly me___ pre-ten-ding that they're

love, no home, nick - el to loan, could it be rea-lly me___ pre-ten-ding that they're

___ that there are some___ with no home,___ not a nick-le to loan,___ could it be rea-lly me___ pre-ten-ding that they're

no home,___ nick - el to loan, not a -

not a - lone. Wil - low___ scarred, bro - ken___ heart, washed out___ dream,___

not a - lone. Wil - low___ scarred, bro - ken___ heart, washed out___ dream,

not a - lone.___ A wil-low deep-ly scarred some-bod-y's brok en heart and a washed out dream,_____ they

-lone. Wil - low___ scarred, bro - ken___ heart, washed out___ dream,

pat - tern,___ wind you see,___ so I'll___ start with me.___

pat - tern,___ wind you see,___ so I'll___ start with me.___

fol-low the pat-tern of the wind you see, 'cause they got no place___ to be that's why I'm start-ing with me.

pat - tern,___ wind you see,___ so I'll___ start with me.___

look at your self and then make a change. look at your self and then make a change. I'm start-ing with the

look at your self and then make a change. look at your self and then make a change. I'm start-ing with the

look at your self and then make a change. look at your self and then make a Start - ing with the

look at your self and then make a change. look at your self and then make a Start - ing with the

man in the mir-ror, I'm ask ing him to change his ways,

man in the mir-ror, I'm ask ing him to change his ways,

man in the mir-ror, ask - ing him to change his ways,

man in the mir-ror, ask - ing him to change his ways,

and no___ mes-sage could have been an - y clear-er: if you wan-na make the world a bet-ter place take a

and no mes-sage could have been an - y clear-er: if you wan-na make the world a bet-ter place take a

and no___ mes-sage could have been an - y clear-er: if you wan-na make the world a bet-ter place take a

no___ mes - sage could be an - y clear-er: if you wan-na make the world a bet-ter place take a

look at your-self and then make the change, you got-ta get it right__while you've got the time_'cause when you

look at your-self and then make the change, you got-ta get it right__while you've got the time_'cause when you

look at your-self and then make the change, you got-ta get it right__while you've got the time_'cause when you

look at your-self and then make the change, you got-ta get it right__while you've got the time_'cause when you

close your heart then you close your mind._____ na na na na na na_____ na na

close your heart then you close your mind._____ na na na na na na_____ na na

close your heart then you close your mind._____ na na na na na na_____ na na

close your heart then you close your mind,_____ mind,_____ mind.___

na na na na_____ na na_____ na na na na na na na na_____ na na na na na na

na na na na_____ na na_____ na na na na na na na na_____ na na na na na na

na na na na_____ na na_____ na na na na na na na na_____ na na na na na na

_____ na na na na na na na_____ na na

456789